EMMANUEL JOSEPH

Digital Gold Rush: Insights into Cryptocurrency Markets

Copyright © 2025 by Emmanuel Joseph

All rights reserved. No part of this publication may be reproduced, stored or transmitted in any form or by any means, electronic, mechanical, photocopying, recording, scanning, or otherwise without written permission from the publisher. It is illegal to copy this book, post it to a website, or distribute it by any other means without permission.

First edition

This book was professionally typeset on Reedsy.
Find out more at reedsy.com

Contents

1	Chapter 1: The Birth of Cryptocurrency	1
2	Chapter 2: The Mechanics of Blockchain Technology	3
3	Chapter 3: The Rise of Altcoins	5
4	Chapter 4: Navigating the Cryptocurrency Market	7
5	Chapter 5: The Role of Regulation	9
6	Chapter 6: Decentralized Finance (DeFi)	11
7	Chapter 7: The Impact of Institutional Investment	13
8	Chapter 8: Cryptocurrency Mining	15
9	Chapter 9: The Social Impact of Cryptocurrency	17
10	Chapter 10: The Future of Cryptocurrency	19
11	Chapter 11: Cryptocurrency and Global Economy	21
12	Chapter 12: Personal Stories and Case Studies	23

1

Chapter 1: The Birth of Cryptocurrency

Cryptocurrency has revolutionized the world of finance, creating a new era of digital assets. This journey began with the mysterious Satoshi Nakamoto, who introduced Bitcoin in 2009. Bitcoin, the first decentralized digital currency, uses blockchain technology to offer a secure and transparent way to transfer value without intermediaries. The birth of cryptocurrency was a response to the shortcomings of traditional financial systems, aiming to provide a more democratic and accessible financial ecosystem.

Bitcoin's success paved the way for the development of thousands of other cryptocurrencies, collectively known as altcoins. Each new cryptocurrency brought unique features and innovations, further expanding the digital asset landscape. Ethereum, for example, introduced smart contracts, enabling developers to build decentralized applications on its platform. This innovation opened up a world of possibilities, from decentralized finance (DeFi) to non-fungible tokens (NFTs).

The early days of cryptocurrency were marked by skepticism and uncertainty. Many people doubted the viability of digital currencies, and regulatory bodies struggled to keep up with the rapid pace of innovation. Despite these challenges, the cryptocurrency market continued to grow, driven by a passionate and dedicated community of developers, investors, and enthusiasts.

As more people became aware of the potential benefits of cryptocurrency, adoption began to increase. Businesses started accepting Bitcoin and other cryptocurrencies as payment, and institutional investors began to take notice. This growing interest and acceptance helped to legitimize the market and laid the foundation for the next phase of growth and development.

2

Chapter 2: The Mechanics of Blockchain Technology

At the heart of every cryptocurrency lies blockchain technology, a decentralized and transparent ledger that records all transactions. Blockchain technology ensures that transactions are secure, tamper-proof, and verifiable. Each block in the chain contains a list of transactions, and once a block is added, it cannot be altered. This immutability is one of the key features that make blockchain technology so powerful.

Blockchain technology operates on a consensus mechanism, which ensures that all participants in the network agree on the validity of transactions. There are several types of consensus mechanisms, including Proof of Work (PoW) and Proof of Stake (PoS). PoW, used by Bitcoin, requires miners to solve complex mathematical problems to validate transactions and add them to the blockchain. PoS, used by Ethereum 2.0, allows validators to create new blocks and validate transactions based on the number of coins they hold and are willing to "stake" as collateral.

One of the most significant advantages of blockchain technology is its transparency. All transactions are recorded on a public ledger, which anyone can access and verify. This transparency helps to prevent fraud and ensures that the system is fair and accountable. Additionally, the decentralized nature of blockchain technology eliminates the need for intermediaries, reducing costs and increasing efficiency.

Blockchain technology has applications far beyond cryptocurrency. It is being used to revolutionize industries such as supply chain management, healthcare, and finance. By providing a secure and transparent way to record and verify transactions, blockchain technology has the potential to transform the way we conduct business and interact with one another.

3

Chapter 3: The Rise of Altcoins

While Bitcoin remains the most well-known cryptocurrency, the rise of altcoins has significantly diversified the digital asset landscape. Altcoins, or alternative cryptocurrencies, refer to any digital currency other than Bitcoin. These digital assets offer unique features and innovations that differentiate them from Bitcoin and each other. Ethereum, for instance, introduced smart contracts, enabling developers to create decentralized applications (dApps) on its platform.

One of the key drivers behind the rise of altcoins is the desire to improve upon the limitations of Bitcoin. For example, Litecoin was created to offer faster transaction times and lower fees, while Ripple focuses on providing a seamless and efficient cross-border payment system for financial institutions. Each altcoin aims to address specific use cases and challenges within the cryptocurrency ecosystem.

The introduction of Initial Coin Offerings (ICOs) and later, Security Token Offerings (STOs), provided a new way for startups and projects to raise funds by issuing their own digital tokens. This fundraising method democratized access to capital and allowed investors to participate in the early stages of innovative projects. However, it also led to a proliferation of altcoins, some of which were created solely to capitalize on the hype and lacked genuine value or utility.

As the altcoin market matured, it became increasingly important for investors to conduct thorough research and due diligence before investing in new projects. Evaluating the team behind a project, its technology, use case, and overall market potential are crucial steps in identifying promising altcoins. Despite the risks, the rise of altcoins has contributed to the growth and diversification of the cryptocurrency market, offering new opportunities and innovations.

4

Chapter 4: Navigating the Cryptocurrency Market

Navigating the cryptocurrency market can be a daunting task for both novice and experienced investors. The market is known for its volatility, with prices often experiencing significant fluctuations within short periods. Understanding the factors that influence these price movements is essential for making informed investment decisions. Key factors include market sentiment, regulatory developments, technological advancements, and macroeconomic trends.

One of the most effective ways to navigate the cryptocurrency market is through diversification. By investing in a range of digital assets, investors can spread their risk and potentially increase their chances of success. Diversification can involve holding a mix of well-established cryptocurrencies like Bitcoin and Ethereum, as well as promising altcoins with strong fundamentals and growth potential. Additionally, investors should stay informed about market trends and news to identify potential opportunities and risks.

Technical analysis is another valuable tool for navigating the cryptocurrency market. This method involves analyzing historical price data and identifying patterns to predict future price movements. Key indicators used in technical analysis include moving averages, relative strength index (RSI), and Bollinger Bands. While technical analysis can provide valuable insights, it is essential to remember that it is not foolproof and should be used in conjunction with other research and analysis methods.

Managing risk is a crucial aspect of navigating the cryptocurrency market. Investors should set clear investment goals, establish a risk tolerance level, and implement strategies such as stop-loss orders to protect their investments. Additionally, it is essential to avoid emotional decision-making and remain disciplined in following a well-thought-out investment plan. By staying informed, diversifying, and managing risk, investors can better navigate the complex and dynamic cryptocurrency market.

5

Chapter 5: The Role of Regulation

Regulation plays a significant role in the cryptocurrency market, shaping its development and influencing investor confidence. Governments and regulatory bodies around the world have adopted varying approaches to cryptocurrency regulation, ranging from outright bans to supportive frameworks that foster innovation. Understanding the regulatory landscape is crucial for investors, developers, and businesses operating within the cryptocurrency ecosystem.

One of the primary concerns for regulators is the potential for cryptocurrencies to be used for illegal activities such as money laundering, terrorist financing, and tax evasion. To address these concerns, many countries have implemented Anti-Money Laundering (AML) and Know Your Customer (KYC) requirements for cryptocurrency exchanges and other service providers. These measures aim to increase transparency and ensure that participants in the market are held accountable.

Regulatory clarity can also benefit the cryptocurrency market by providing a clear framework for businesses and investors to operate within. For example, the introduction of the General Data Protection Regulation (GDPR) in the European Union has provided guidelines for how personal data should be handled, increasing trust and confidence in digital services. Similarly, clear regulations on the issuance and trading of digital tokens can help protect investors and promote the growth of legitimate projects.

Despite the potential benefits of regulation, there is a delicate balance between fostering innovation and ensuring consumer protection. Overly restrictive regulations can stifle growth and drive innovation to more favorable jurisdictions, while a lack of regulation can lead to market manipulation and fraud. As the cryptocurrency market continues to evolve, regulators must work closely with industry stakeholders to develop balanced and effective regulatory frameworks.

6

Chapter 6: Decentralized Finance (DeFi)

Decentralized Finance (DeFi) represents one of the most exciting and rapidly growing sectors within the cryptocurrency market. DeFi leverages blockchain technology to create a wide range of financial services and products that are open, transparent, and accessible to anyone with an internet connection. By eliminating intermediaries, DeFi aims to provide more efficient and inclusive financial solutions.

One of the key components of DeFi is decentralized lending and borrowing platforms. These platforms allow users to lend their digital assets to others in exchange for interest or to borrow assets by providing collateral. Smart contracts automate the process, ensuring that loans are secure and terms are enforced without the need for intermediaries. This innovation has the potential to democratize access to credit and provide more competitive interest rates compared to traditional financial institutions.

Decentralized exchanges (DEXs) are another essential element of the DeFi ecosystem. Unlike centralized exchanges, DEXs operate without a central authority, allowing users to trade directly with one another. This peer-to-peer trading model enhances security and reduces the risk of hacking or fraud. Additionally, DEXs often offer lower fees and greater privacy compared to their centralized counterparts.

The DeFi ecosystem also includes a wide range of other financial products and services, such as yield farming, stablecoins, and decentralized insurance.

Yield farming involves providing liquidity to DeFi protocols in exchange for rewards, while stablecoins are digital assets pegged to stable assets like fiat currencies to reduce volatility. Decentralized insurance platforms use smart contracts to provide coverage for various risks, offering a more transparent and efficient alternative to traditional insurance.

7

Chapter 7: The Impact of Institutional Investment

Institutional investment has played a significant role in legitimizing and driving the growth of the cryptocurrency market. Over the past few years, an increasing number of institutional investors, such as hedge funds, family offices, and publicly traded companies, have entered the market. This influx of institutional capital has brought greater credibility, liquidity, and stability to the market.

One of the key factors driving institutional investment in cryptocurrency is the potential for significant returns. As traditional assets like stocks and bonds face diminishing returns, institutional investors are increasingly looking to diversify their portfolios with significant returns. As traditional assets like stocks and bonds face diminishing returns, institutional investors are increasingly looking to diversify their portfolios with alternative assets, including cryptocurrencies. The potential for high returns, coupled with the growing acceptance of digital assets, has made cryptocurrencies an attractive investment option.

The entry of institutional investors has also led to the development of new financial products and services tailored to their needs. For example, cryptocurrency custodians offer secure storage solutions for large amounts of digital assets, addressing concerns about security and theft. Additionally, the introduction of regulated cryptocurrency investment funds and exchange-traded products has made it easier for institutions to gain exposure to the market.

Another significant impact of institutional investment is the increase in market liquidity. The influx of capital from institutional investors has led to higher trading volumes and greater market depth, reducing the impact of large trades on price fluctuations. This increased liquidity has made the market more attractive to both retail and institutional investors, further driving growth and adoption.

The involvement of institutional investors has also brought greater scrutiny and regulatory oversight to the cryptocurrency market. As institutions adhere to strict regulatory standards, their participation has encouraged the development of more transparent and compliant market practices. This, in turn, has helped to build trust and confidence in the market, attracting even more participants and fostering long-term growth.

8

Chapter 8: Cryptocurrency Mining

Cryptocurrency mining is the process by which new digital assets are created and transactions are verified on the blockchain. This process involves solving complex mathematical problems, which require significant computational power. Miners compete to solve these problems, and the first to do so is rewarded with newly created cryptocurrency and transaction fees.

Bitcoin mining, for example, uses the Proof of Work (PoW) consensus mechanism, which requires miners to perform energy-intensive calculations. This process ensures the security and integrity of the Bitcoin network, but it has also raised concerns about its environmental impact. To address these concerns, some newer cryptocurrencies have adopted alternative consensus mechanisms, such as Proof of Stake (PoS), which are less energy-intensive.

The mining process has evolved significantly since the early days of cryptocurrency. Initially, individuals could mine Bitcoin using their personal computers. However, as the network grew and the difficulty of mining increased, specialized hardware known as Application-Specific Integrated Circuits (ASICs) became necessary to remain competitive. Today, large mining farms with hundreds or thousands of ASICs dominate the industry, making it increasingly difficult for individual miners to participate.

Despite the challenges, mining remains an essential component of the cryptocurrency ecosystem. It provides a decentralized way to secure and validate transactions, ensuring the integrity of the network. Additionally, mining can be a profitable venture for those with access to affordable electricity and efficient hardware. As the cryptocurrency market continues to evolve, mining practices and technologies will likely continue to adapt and innovate.

9

Chapter 9: The Social Impact of Cryptocurrency

Cryptocurrencies have the potential to create significant social impact by providing financial inclusion and empowering individuals in underserved communities. Traditional financial systems often exclude large segments of the population, particularly in developing countries, due to factors such as lack of access to banking infrastructure, high fees, and stringent requirements. Cryptocurrencies offer a decentralized and accessible alternative, enabling anyone with an internet connection to participate in the global economy.

One of the most notable examples of cryptocurrency's social impact is its use in remittances. Millions of people around the world rely on remittances from family members working abroad to support their livelihoods. Traditional remittance services are often expensive and slow, with fees eating into the funds sent. Cryptocurrencies provide a faster and more cost-effective solution, allowing people to send money across borders with minimal fees and delays.

Cryptocurrencies also have the potential to empower individuals by giving them greater control over their financial assets. In countries with unstable economies or oppressive regimes, people may face restrictions on accessing or transferring their funds. Cryptocurrencies offer a way to circumvent these restrictions, providing a secure and transparent means of storing and transferring value. This financial autonomy can help individuals protect their wealth and achieve greater economic independence.

Additionally, blockchain technology can be used to address social challenges beyond financial inclusion. For example, blockchain-based platforms can enhance transparency and accountability in supply chains, ensuring that products are ethically sourced and produced. Similarly, blockchain can be used to improve the delivery of humanitarian aid by ensuring that funds are distributed efficiently and reach those in need. As the technology continues to develop, its potential to create positive social impact will likely expand.

10

Chapter 10: The Future of Cryptocurrency

The future of cryptocurrency is filled with potential and possibilities, as the technology continues to evolve and mature. One of the most significant trends shaping the future of cryptocurrency is the growing interest in decentralized finance (DeFi). DeFi aims to recreate traditional financial systems using blockchain technology, offering a wide range of financial services such as lending, borrowing, and trading without intermediaries. This innovation has the potential to revolutionize the financial industry, making it more inclusive, transparent, and efficient.

Another important trend is the increasing integration of cryptocurrency into mainstream financial systems. Central banks around the world are exploring the concept of central bank digital currencies (CBDCs), which are digital versions of traditional fiat currencies. CBDCs aim to combine the benefits of digital currencies with the stability and trust of traditional financial systems. If successfully implemented, CBDCs could further legitimize digital currencies and drive widespread adoption.

The development of new and innovative use cases for blockchain technology will also play a crucial role in shaping the future of cryptocurrency. Beyond financial applications, blockchain has the potential to transform industries such as healthcare, supply chain management, and voting systems. By providing secure, transparent, and efficient solutions, blockchain technology can address many of the challenges faced by these industries and create new opportunities for growth and innovation.

However, the future of cryptocurrency is not without challenges. Regulatory uncertainty remains a significant hurdle, as governments and regulatory bodies continue to grapple with how to best oversee and manage the rapidly evolving market. Additionally, the environmental impact of energy-intensive consensus mechanisms like Proof of Work must be addressed to ensure the sustainability of the technology.

Despite these challenges, the future of cryptocurrency looks promising. As the technology continues to develop and mature, it has the potential to create a more inclusive, transparent, and efficient global economy. By embracing innovation and addressing the challenges ahead, the cryptocurrency market can continue to grow and thrive, shaping the future of finance and beyond.

11

Chapter 11: Cryptocurrency and Global Economy

The impact of cryptocurrency on the global economy is profound and far-reaching. Cryptocurrencies have introduced new dynamics to the financial system, challenging traditional banking and financial institutions. By providing a decentralized and borderless alternative to traditional currencies, cryptocurrencies have the potential to reshape global trade and finance.

One of the most significant impacts of cryptocurrency on the global economy is the democratization of finance. Cryptocurrencies provide access to financial services for individuals and businesses that may be excluded from traditional financial systems. This inclusivity can drive economic growth and development, particularly in regions with limited access to banking infrastructure.

Cryptocurrencies also facilitate cross-border transactions, reducing the need for intermediaries and lowering transaction costs. This can enhance global trade and commerce by making it easier and more cost-effective for businesses to conduct transactions with international partners. Additionally, cryptocurrencies can provide a hedge against currency fluctuations and economic instability, offering a more stable store of value for individuals and businesses in volatile economies.

The rise of cryptocurrency has also spurred innovation and competition within the financial industry. Traditional financial institutions are increasingly exploring blockchain technology and digital assets to improve their services and remain competitive. This has led to the development of new financial products and services, such as digital wallets, blockchain-based payment systems, and tokenized assets.

However, the integration of cryptocurrency into the global economy also presents challenges. Regulatory uncertainty, market volatility, and security concerns must be addressed to ensure the stability and sustainability of the cryptocurrency market. Additionally, the environmental impact of cryptocurrency mining and the energy consumption of blockchain networks must be considered as the technology continues to evolve.

Overall, the impact of cryptocurrency on the global economy is both transformative and challenging. As the technology continues to develop and mature, it has the potential to create a more inclusive, efficient, and innovative financial system. By addressing the challenges and embracing the opportunities, the global economy can benefit from the transformative power of cryptocurrency.

12

Chapter 12: Personal Stories and Case Studies

The world of cryptocurrency is filled with personal stories and case studies that highlight its transformative potential and the impact it can have on individuals and communities. These stories provide valuable insights into the real-world applications of cryptocurrency and the ways in which it can create positive change.

One notable case study is the story of BitPesa, a fintech startup based in Kenya. BitPesa uses blockchain technology to provide faster and more affordable cross-border payment solutions for businesses and individuals in Africa. By leveraging cryptocurrency, BitPesa has been able to reduce the cost and time associated with traditional remittance services, empowering small businesses and promoting economic growth in the region.

Another inspiring story is that of Venezuelan citizens who have turned to cryptocurrency as a means of survival amid the country's economic crisis. With hyperinflation rendering the national currency nearly worthless, many Venezuelans have adopted cryptocurrencies like Bitcoin to preserve their wealth and access essential goods and services. This grassroots adoption of cryptocurrency demonstrates its potential to provide financial stability and independence in times of crisis.

The story of Ethereum co-founder Vitalik Buterin is also worth mentioning.

Born in Russia and raised in Canada, Buterin was introduced to Bitcoin at a young age and quickly recognized its potential. In 2013, he proposed the idea of Ethereum, a decentralized platform that enables the creation of smart contracts and decentralized applications. Today, Ethereum is one of the most influential and widely used blockchain platforms, with applications spanning finance, gaming, supply chain management, and more.

These personal stories and case studies illustrate the diverse and impactful ways in which cryptocurrency is being used around the world. From fostering financial inclusion and economic growth to providing a lifeline in times of crisis, cryptocurrency has the potential to create positive change and transform lives. As the technology continues to evolve, more stories of innovation and empowerment will undoubtedly emerge, showcasing the transformative power of cryptocurrency.

www.ingramcontent.com/pod-product-compliance
Lightning Source LLC
LaVergne TN
LVHW020743090526
838202LV00057BA/6200